TRANSPOSIUM

TRANSPOSIUM

Dani Yourukova

AUCKLAND
UNIVERSITY
PRESS

First published 2023
Auckland University Press
University of Auckland
Private Bag 92019
Auckland 1142
New Zealand
www.aucklanduniversitypress.co.nz

ISBN 978 1 77671 1 000

A catalogue record for this book is available from the National Library of New Zealand

Cover design by Philip Kelly
Internal design by Amy Tansell, WordsAlive Ltd
Cover image: an adaptation of Paul Richer's *Tres In Una*, Salon of 1913, public domain via Wikimedia Commons.

This book was printed on FSC® certified paper

Printed in China by Everbest Printing Investment Ltd

The Symposium is the dialogue of the conflict between philosophy and poetry where the poets are in a position to defend themselves.

— Leo Strauss

CONTENTS

III ALCIBIADES CHOOSES THEIR OWN ADVENTURE

I

TRANSPOSIUM

Symposium (Adapted)

/sɪmˈpəʊzɪəm/

noun

1. a conference or meeting to discuss a particular subject.
2. a drinking party or convivial discussion, especially as held in ancient Greece after a banquet (and notable as the title of a work by Plato).

You must answer all questions to the best of your abilities. We
will judge you by your answers
, and the questions that you ask
or don't   the level of   intellectual rigour
you display   your
variations in tone and   medium.
So ask yourself   what it means
to look inside a person   and
tag yourself
assign a colour to your   taste in men
beverage order   favoured song lyric   unlock your
Barbie movie sidekick   choose a
philosophical position   reveal your
sun sign   past life   gender expression
and then construct
a micro-identity   around the
answer   the question:

What the fuck is wrong with you?

a) I act without thinking things through
b) Rampant misogyny
c) No bitches
d) I use jokes to conceal my devastating loneliness
e) Sometimes I cry at the moon
f) I'm a Devil's Advocate piece of garbage   [This is the right answer]
g) Absolutely nothing

3

Do you want a glass of wine?

a) I would prefer to open a convivial discussion on the nature of Eros
b) No thank you, I'm actually pretty hungover right now
c) Did you know that drinking alcohol is bad for you?
d) Do you have water or something?
e) Sure, maybe a little
f) I could go either way   [This is the right answer]
g) I'M ALREADY THERE BAYBEE I'M
   POURING YOU ALL DRINKS RIGHT NOW

What is your most unpopular opinion?

a) Achilles was a Bottom
b) Heterosexuality is disgusting
c) Plants experience Eros
d) The ideal human shape is spherical
   (with four hands and as many legs, and two faces on opposite sides of a single head)
e) A e s t h e t i c s
f) All human beings are both physically and
   mentally pregnant at all times.   [This is the right answer]
g) Listen, why won't Socrates have sex with me??

How will you be remembered?

a) I won't
b) Rancid vibes
c) Dead
d) Something that I never actually said will be taken out of context and attributed to
   me, thereby eclipsing an entire lifetime of my professional output as a writer
e) Catalogue of rain sounds
f) Discourse   [This is the right answer]
g) A monument to my perfect ass

What is Love?

a) The homoerotic clash of sweaty bodies
b) I'm a sapiosexual
c) Fatal medical condition
d) A backpack full of hammers
e) When the last line of a poem goes really hard, illuminating all that has come before it in a way that is somehow both unexpected and inevitable
f) A really complicated ladder   [This is the right answer]
g) BABY DON'T HURT ME

If you answered mostly . . .

A: turn to page 7
B: turn to page 9
C: turn to page 11
D: turn to page 13
E: turn to page 15
F: turn to page 16
G: turn to page 19

If you can establish no viable or replicable pattern to your answers
you have failed.

Turn to page XXXX

You are . . .

PHAEDRUS

They sent Orpheus the son of Oeagrus
away from Hades unsatisfied.
They regarded him as soft.
He wasn't brave enough to die
but contrived to enter Hades alive,
so they had him die at the hands of women.
Whereas Achilles, they rewarded.

When Achilles discovered that all his killing
would in turn cause his own death,
he was brave enough to stand
by his lover Patroclus, die *for* Patroclus,
and keep on killing.
Aeschylus is a fool when he claims
that Achilles was Patroclus's ~~erastes~~ Top.
He was much more attractive, and
much younger than Patroclus,
as Homer records.

Gods are more amazed
and impressed
by the love that a Bottom has for a Top.
Tops are all possessed by *Eros*,
Bottoms have to act alone.
That is why they honoured Achilles more
by letting him go.

If this doesn't sound like you, turn back to page 3. Take the quiz again.

You are . . .

PAUSANIAS

being gay isn't a competition but / you're winning
you imagine that there are / two kinds of love and

lovers / two Aphrodites
the Common, born of Zeus and Dione / and the Celestial

as born from / the blood of Ouranos
Celestial Aphrodite / has no origin

in sex between woman and man, though / there is
nothing much of woman about her / (a femme king)

and this is why you worship him / at her altar
with the quiet grasping of a / man who says

'Gold Star Gay' / unironically

Agathon, who holds your heart
will leave for Macedonia
in ten years' time
and you will follow him.
You will follow him for
the rest of your life.

If this doesn't sound like you, turn back to page 3. Take the quiz again.

You are . . .

ERYXIMACHUS

You like to go home early from every party,
when it passes a particular hour. Specifically,

the hour of carrying balloon animals around in your chest,
and walking in on people you don't know

doing vodka shots out of White Aladdin's belly button.
The body is the origin point . . . .

of embarrassment,
like the vestigial nipple,

it is an uneasy relationship
between the trans body

and the medical profession,
to participate is to become garden moss

to spring genially beneath the heel
of a gardener unfamiliar

with your genus.
The body is an outpouring

of humours, and fluids, and grief. To love is
to heave that body against a foreign shore

and hope for the best.

If this doesn't sound like you, turn back to page 3. Take the quiz again.

You are . . .

ARISTOPHANES

Let's talk about love!
At a party full of pre-established couples   and also you.

Like standing in front of a derelict lighthouse
and setting yourself on fire,
in the hope that someone might notice you
          . . . . this time.

Like cutting an egg in half
with a strand of hair
at a knife festival,
or finding a cave painting of a broken telephone.

Why love someone when you could
write a deranged little problem
into the world, instead?

Which is more like whispering 'you are my other half' to
the person that you have been experiencing extended
sexual tension with across several compelling seasons of television
and just as they lean in to respond
. . . .

you lose both of your legs in a tragic and totally avoidable
boating accident.

Maybe you should have kept your eyes on the sea.

If this doesn't sound like you, turn back to page 3. Take the quiz again.

You are . . .

AGATHON

To speak in praise of love is no small task,
sweet Agathon, let all your words alight
on Eros. Young, attractive, good (and masc).
An artist! Wreathed in beauty, ever-bright

who steps in mind so slight he goes untouched,
and into Psyche's bower quiet crept,
love's blessing softly granted under such
unstirred seas, stilled breeze, where cares have slept.

But love can live (and should) without applause.
What meaning does a lyric then impart?
To praise or blame? To queer or cause?
The crowd goes WILD, and Agathon departs.

The beauty of love, *Philosophia* calls,
see how Eros makes a poet of us all.

If this doesn't sound like you, turn back to page 3. Take the quiz again.

You are . . .

~~SOCRATES~~ CORRECT

If we are to understand Love's purpose as the permanent possession of goodness for oneself, then we need to ask under what conditions and in what sphere of activity the determination and energy of people with this purpose may be called 'Love'.

Would you accept, Phaedrus, a speech that is true and tumbles out in any old order?

If Socrates is to give an account of love that was related to him by a priestess from Mantinea, what is the probability that 'Diotima' is Socrates' deadname?

If the Socratic Method leaves Athens at 9.04 a.m., averaging 98 mph and another train headed in the same direction leaves Sparta at 1.15 p.m., averaging 113 mph

to the nearest tenth, how many hours after the second train leaves
will society crumble?

If sex is a kind of birth,
then how many underground sewer systems are haunted by the ghosts of
Victorian schoolchildren?

If three trans people walk into a Discord server, how long will it take before someone changes their screen name to   'sexy ritalin prescription'?

If Love is an open door   why haven't we monetised doorstops yet?

If Love is all you need   why NOT overthrow capitalism at the earliest convenience?

If Love is a losing game,
                              why is anyone playing???

If Plato loves Socrates so much, why doesn't he   XXXXXXXXXXXXXX

Don't you realise XXXXXXXX that, as long as it isn't supported XXXXXXXX by a justification, true belief ISN'T knowledge XXXXXXXXXXXXX but isn't ignorance either? That in fact XXXX true belief is an *intermediate* area XXXXXX between knowledge and ignorance?

Can you explain that XXXXXXXX to me one more time?

XXXXXXX
XX

XXXXXXXXX
XXXXX

Feels good to be validated by arbitrary systems of classification, doesn't it? Do it again.
Turn to page XXXX.

You are . . .

ALCIBIADES

her eyes are wide enough to drink from as we slide together on the floor / the length of her hand in my hair / the music a thrum that pulses / through the tendons in her neck / I'm forgetting that I came here with someone else / who makes me laugh / but can't make me cum / whose best friend is much hotter than he is / isn't it lucky that I can't see them anymore / in the dark crush of bodies / *I don't wanna be your friend* / there's something about the timing / *I just wanna be your lover* / the taut feel of a chord progression / wanting to come home / that makes me want to kiss her / in this pick of sparks and struck nerves / and anguished winks in the dark / I'm always doing this / can't seem to articulate / the difference between wanting / being wanted / my compulsive need to create the most satisfying narrative conclusion / to every problem / she skims a slow kiss across the shell of my ear / too much and not enough / as I feel the salt-white swoop / of her throat / against my mouth

If this doesn't sound like you, turn back to page 3. Take the quiz again.

II

DIALECTIC

Dark Academia

you are ink-stained shirt sleeves and
clenched complexes,
cobblestones and tartan skirts,
and most importantly, you are
mine
       mine
            mine,

you are a minimum of
three hundred years old and deeply haunted
by a culture of class-centric white elitism,
but in   a sexy way
like the ghost of Prince Philip crying
in a strip club, or
wearing fishnets to a fox hunt.

you haunt me so grievously
that I am forced to develop a fetish
for the generous curvature of ancient vases,
so intense,
that each time the bell rings
I am compelled to find a quiet room in the museum
sit behind long glass panes
the air slow and swollen with time,
and make eye contact with Plato across a selection of attic black-figure glazed ware.
      there you are

I take out the orange I was saving specifically for this occasion
heft it threateningly in my palm
and think, *that smooth mother fucker,*
when he doesn't flinch.

then, I peel the rind with my teeth, never breaking our mutual gaze,
and strip the lines of my tweed suit from the branches
of my body in transgressive, horn-rimmed ecstasy.
I will stay there until someone with a vacuum cleaner shows up,
totally devastating my sense of worth and ability to pay my tuition fees,
buy a gun made out of pop culture references
and kill myself, with a melodramatic cartoon *bang*.

o Dark Academia . . .
it makes me want to hit you with an urn
and write a sonnet about the process.

it makes me want to push you over the edge of a cliff
and – as you hang precipitously –
dismantle all of your power structures
and by power structures, I do mean
hands.

I hate you so much I want to build a monument to you
tastefully rendered, in the blood concrete of Martian
colonies,

I hate you so much that I invest in a poorly planned
lower back tattoo, and send you photos of the evidence,

I hate you
I hate you
I hate you so much

I whisper, before stitching your name
into my elbow patches and setting an antique clock
on fire.

and when the ashes settle, I send a little note,
telling you that I have done this,
and asking what you think?
was it too much?
because I can dial it back if you think
                              it was too much.

Goodreads accessing the communal mind to deliver a balanced review of Plato's *Symposium* (385 –370 BCE)

A found poem

The party is over
★★☆☆☆

I am outraged after reading this.

First, the approach that was taken (multiple layers of theory of mind) opposed the main topic, love.

Why the hell am I, as the reader, supposed to believe what comes from the grapevine;

        everyone was DRUNK

Plato and his crew were sketchy mother fuckers

Philosophers, all the way down
★★★★★

Plato crafts narrative devices

story within a story within a story within a story

the cornerstone of understanding is

engaging in dialogue

Love,
        separated from beauty.

Love

      in relation to philosophy . . .

or perhaps more so

the use of the libido – and how one succeeds in perception of the forms

immersed in the mysteries

Eyes are the window to the soul

★★★★☆

embarrassed to admit I was picturing alcibiades as timothée chalamet

No, but what does it mean
★★★★★

The central question in Plato's *Symposium*.

The Magnificent Hepta (Phaedrus, Pausanias, Eryximachus, Aristophanes, Agathon, Socrates and Alcibiades)

Dayum, these guys knew how to throw a party.

Plato via Aristophanes via Hedwig and the Angry Inch

★★★★☆

We wrapped our arms around each other
Tried to shove ourselves back together
We were making love, making love
It was a cold dark evening such a long time ago
When by the mighty hand of jove
It was a sad story how we became lonely two-legged creatures
The story, the origin of love
That's the origin of love

Socrates. The man. The myth. The literary construct.
★★★★★

This is so very good

Really

It's obviously very important

Aristophanes has maybe the best section

Alcibiades is almost as good

              an eternal dinner party of the gods . . .

Socrates (drinks everyone under the table and never gets drunk) blows up all the spots with his last monologue

which only goes to show why he's Socrates . . .

Someone notices Plato's relation to the text
★★☆☆☆

I'm just not a fan of Plato I guess / None of his stuff really makes sense to me / he flips around saying something is true / because it's true / doesn't ever give any real proof / I think if I were Socrates I would not have wanted Plato putting words in my mouth / Furthermore / I think anyone that gave anything Plato wrote more than two stars / probably didn't read it

It's not nothing
★☆☆☆☆

Some useful tips on curing hiccups.

Phaedrus Recites a Catalogue of Ships

1. The Ship of Theseus is a well-known metaphysical experiment on the question of identity. As the ship decays against the tides, the Athenians replace the boards, trying to keep the wreck alive, rotting boards pried from healthy flesh.

2. This is a necessary step from the shipwright's perspective, but the philosopher-in-training is less interested in the process and more interested in the consequences: At which point does the ship become a different ship? Are we a collection of parts, or are we something else?

3. *I will tell the Lords of the ships and the ship's numbers. / Leitos and Peneleos were leaders of the Boiotians, / with Arkesilaos and Prothoenor and Klonios;*

4. Excavations in the Athenian Agora have brought to light fragments of three sculpted ophthalmoi, designed to be affixed to the prows of ships. Three hypotheses are offered to explain the presence of nautical artifacts within the Agora:
   a) they may have served as honorific fixtures relating to the fleet,
   b) represented surplus naval equipment stored in the Strategeion, or
   c) belonged to a wheeled ship used in the Anthesteria or the Greater Panathenaia festival.

5. Please imagine the following: the prow of Theseus's ship surging through the waves of the wine-dark sea, adorned with marble-carved googly eyes, irises the size of dinner plates.

6. This is a dream that an Athenian once had.

7. Your mother's car has always looked a little embarrassed to you, headlights dipped, grille rattling a bracketed grin.

8. The word for this is *apophenia*.

9. We have longed to put faces on machines for thousands of years.

10. *they who lived in Hyria and in rocky Aulis, / in the hill bends of Eteneos, and Schoinos, and Skolos / Thespeia and Graia, and in spacious Mykalessos*

11. The term 'apophenia' was used by Klaus Conrad to characterise an early symptom of schizophrenia. He defined it as 'unmotivated seeing of connections [accompanied by] a specific feeling of abnormal meaningfulness' but the term has softened around the edges. It has come to imply a human inclination to seek patterns in the world around us, to see connection between spaces, and shifts in the random. To see faces in constellations, drawn between the features of inanimate objects.

12. There is a Bulgarian proverb my mother used to say to me: *I can see the ships in your eyes*. It means *You are lying and I can tell*.

13. It feels safe to me. To categorise things, to list and expound and explain them. To order a world around the consequences, extracting meaning from structures, like water from a hose.

14. *they who dwelt about Harma and Eilesion and Erythrai, / they who held Eleon and Hyle and Peteon, / with Okalea and Medeon, the strong-founded citadel,*

15. Briseis is seven years old and comes home from a day with her father. Now that she is back beneath the roof of her mother she is asked where she has been that day.

16. Okay, but what about after that?

17. And how long did that take?

18. You were gone for hours.

19. Where exactly were you and when, you know that I don't have time for this.

20. *I can see the ships in your eyes.*

21. It is difficult sometimes, to keep your eyes above the water.

22. *Kopai, and Eutresis, and Thisbe of the dove-cotes; / they who held Koroneia, and the meadows of Haliartos, / they who held Plataia, and they who dwelt about Glisa,*

23. I have never been able to verify my memory of the Bulgarian proverb 'I can see the ships in your eyes.' I do not know the words my mother would have to speak *na bŭlgarski* to form this phrase, I do not know if it is cultural, regional, localised to the members of our family, or localised to my own imagination. All I have is the outline of a ship. The memorial trace of a howl.

24. Has anyone ever touched you?

25. It is when you are seven years old, or five, or nine. Time perhaps does not have the rigidity that it develops as you grow older, cracking like a tree root over earth.

26. *they who held the lower Thebes, the strong-founded citadel, / and Onchestos the sacred, the shining grove of Poseidon;*

27. When you were in the garden dreaming, when you were in the garden telling stories to yourself, when you watched, underground, when you crept, when you made potions from dirt and sap, fuchsia buds squeezed, pollen dabbed, petals stretched past breaking, veins of vibrant green and sycamore sweet, how long were you in the garden?

28. Now answer the question again, but this time, she says, you'll be taken away if you are wrong.

29. *they who held Arne of the great vineyards, and Mideia, / with Nisa the sacrosanct and uttermost Anthedon.*

30. This is because she loves you, your mother explains. She needs to know what your father might have done to you, and she says the same thing when a stain is discovered behind a wicker chair, wide and white and cloying. It seems sometimes that you are always being called to account, and memory fails you over, over again. You shed time like other people shed skin. You cannot, at this point in your life, imagine what she thinks your father might have done to you.

31. *I can see ships in your eyes.*

32. Does it seem plausible to you that the eyes can reveal truth that memory cannot produce?

33. *Of these there were fifty ships in all, and on board / each of these a hundred and twenty sons of the Boiotians.*

34. You wonder if Briseis watched the ships.

35. *But they who lived in Aspledon and Orchomenos of the Minyai, / Askalaphos led these, and Ialmenos, children of Ares, / whom Astyoche bore to him in the house of Aktor*

36. The child Briseis is fussy with her possessions, sullen in the face of mishandling, bringing a red rush to her fair cheeks.

37. When her new stepbrother is introduced to her, he is eight and she is five, and when he uses her felt-tip pens he leaves the lids off, scattered. Fallen like Trojan warriors.

38. Of course he does not want to play with a five-year-old girl, a stranger. He endures her with muted spite. Briseis in turn resents him, because now when she picks up her pen she is left rasping dry where once she could make coloured lines fly across blank space.

39. Her retaliatory rage is deemed hostile, childish and sour, and the assessment is not untrue.

40. She cannot remember the exact point at which she told her mother she didn't want to see him again. She remembers only that childish feelings were not a sufficient condition for curtailing what boys did to you.

41. *Azeus's son, a modest maiden; she went into the chamber / with strong Ares, who was laid in bed with her secretly.*

42. He is sent to her attic, where she has taken to hiding her pens. She keeps neat rows of pencils, glitter and folded notes, ordered by colour and size, in a wooden drawer, on a desk built from boxed things and old planks. The exposed Pink Batts between beams, jaws like the maw of some great beast.

43. He shows her the lighter he keeps in his pocket. He tells her that he will burn her ship to the ground unless she puts her tongue in his mouth. He flicks the flint wheel because he is bored, and to show her that he can.

44. Briseis's mother strokes the child's fair cheeks, whispers *dearest, no one will like you if you cry so much* into the soft wisp of her hair.

45. *With these two were marshalled thirty hollow vessels. / Scheidos and Epistrophos led the men of Phokis, / children of Iphitos, who was son of great-hearted Naubolos.*

46. How sure, can you ever be sure, how firm can you stand in your own perceptions when they have always refused to be reliable?

47. Maybe all children are insufficiently loved.

48. You are being replaced slowly, so slowly that it's almost impossible to tell the difference, but you wonder how much of you will remain when you

are done. How much of you will be given to the next one, to the next one, to the next one.

49. It has taken many years for the ships to stop burning.

50. You can see the ships in your eyes as they lie to you.

The Sims is a two-player game (always has been)

1.
The first creation is the nuclear family
Let there be simulated life!
made from the stuff of middle-class dreams:
golden ratios and gabled windows,
Mum builds with grand design, and indoor flow,
spinning furiously like a funnel spider,
spinning out days
of looking up cheats on GameFAQs,
so that her children will never get older.
She cradles her belly with a restless hand
      and a sideways mouth.

2.
Tom calls me every day
just to talk, for hours, and
my grandma winks   unknowingly.

When he and I create ourselves we say goodbye to
he   and she   as best we can
given the ample 2004 system limitations.
We pay careful attention to astrology
our bodies grown in data   and out of flesh,
in the place where sexy people with genders want to kiss us
my philtrum sticky with fear-sweat

we play at 2 a.m. so Mum won't see.

3.
Renée crafts a mansion-commune and
slams everything on fast forward: a radical act of
free will for our digital selves.

Renée's sim makes a life for herself.
My sim writes a book   then cries
at least Rowan's and Hannah's sims got to make out in the hot tub
bodies stiff-locked in a bubbling tryst.
We watch them, holding our breaths,
like hands held under sheets
before nothing happens.

4.
Jem is a classic serial killer,
loves to burn it all down, crushed flat
in a Murphy bed, mauled by chickens,
aged geriatrics, falling victim to fatally athletic WooHoos.

No ladder in the swimming pool?

            . . . . groundbreaking

the 'florals for spring' of murder,

and! And!
There's not even ROOM for a swimming pool in
this
custom-built vampire-feeding cell block!
. . . .

Amateurs.

5.
When I play again with Mum, the family is nuclear
and the simulation has   taken a turn
for the worse.

There is no robust legal system in
        The Sims 2 (2004). Only monochromatic burglars
being marched into custody
        there can be no custody for us, but

what Mum *can* do is shack Dad up with a waxen
replica   of his family court lawyer,

watch them slowly unravel under strain, the
green stink lines
        serving a savage metaphor,

a rampant breaking down of order,
pizza decaying, meaty slabs of regret

as the bills go stale in the mailbox.

One day, they leave the baby on the kitchen floor,
and she screams and screams

until we stop.

Love poem for *Jurassic Park* (1993)

careful with me, I am easily frightened
        said the sign clipped to the cat cage,
        next to the name the staff have tried to give her.

But Mum always called her 'Jurassic Park'
        because she was 65 million years in the making,
        with her velociraptor shrieks, whiskers trembling,

eyes enormous in the gloom of a grey carpet,
        grey-lit waiting room, waiting
        for anyone to love her, which we did.

Now this is the part in the poem where I should tell you
        about the movie *Jurassic Park* (1993) and how I love that too,
        in order to connect it to the premise of the poem

but, tragically, I have never loved the movie *Jurassic Park* (1993).
        All of the humans were annoying,
        Jeff Goldblum wasn't even hot until like, age 60,

and none of the dinosaurs did anything wrong!
        Except be dead when someone wanted them.

We took her to the vet on the day she didn't die,
        and they told us that her wound would have to stay open:
        clean out twice daily, by hand, with saline solution

I've always been squeamish,
        too afraid to find open flesh and broken things,
        but I learn to bear witness

to the raw red edges of her,
        skin loose like worn elastic,
        to hold this sack of hair and flesh

hissing in the yowling stream
        as salt washes silt
        from a corrugated flap of skin,

debris of necrotic flesh
        rolling cretaceously down the plug,
        so that dinosaurs could walk again.

Pausanias Explains My Sexuality to Me

You are obviously very attracted to me
my best friend's polyamorous Tinder Dom reveals
in a deeply inauspicious WhatsApp message.
It is a complex matter, to query the truth of this suggestion.
On the one hand, I am quite certain
that I have never been attracted to my best friend's polyamorous Tinder Dom,
but on the other hand,
      have I not been wrong before?

I value the act of questioning,
just enough to try,
a chorus of ex-boyfriends applauding my emotional growth,
      really coming out of her shell,
as I am brought to rope-class for kinksters   (Girl Guides for gimps)
upstairs and co-shared with a kickboxing club,
socked feet meet crash mats in glib Biro-blue.
The rope couples are so normal, they're boring,
standing there in their bare arms and activewear
having a good time!!

It makes me think un-erotic thoughts
about karate class with my stepdad when I was twelve, and awful,
hoping to break a brick with my bare hands,
wondering if it would hurt.

When I am roped, my flesh puffs grossly,
my skin pink and throbbing with thwarted blood,
fat rendered into introspective Bratwurst,
bursting at the ends,
cold, on my knees, in a gym, on a Wednesday.

The body adapts to stress,
to the compulsion to say *yes,*
to open eyes, inert body, indexing ceiling tiles,
mouths sucking wetly over mouths,
carpet grain carved into cheek.
        Have I ever really been attracted to anyone?

I ponder the question in a polyester sweat-sheen,
kinkshaming my own limp desire
to read a book and refuse to fuck anybody.

The weeks stretch long as latex,
as I dither over the block button,
like a cat who can't get comfortable.

It takes so long that my best friend
breaks up with their polyamorous Tinder Dom,
and suggests that I might enjoy a weighted blanket instead?

I add one to my rope-free cart
before some cut-price cargo-shorts Daddy Dom can tell me
        You need to be more active in the kink community.

Gender, no. Woman, hot: A Dialectic Executed to Reveal the Nonbinary Lesbian

When we begin, we do not exactly begin at the beginning. Instead we begin with a
   question:

   'What is a nonbinary lesbian, and how do we articulate the way that diverse
   experiences with gender intersect with queer sexuality?'

The esteemed flock of Trans Philosophers deliberate. But it is only after many hours
   of discord
that any sense of consensus is reached. The founding principle is articulated thus:

   Gender, no. Woman, hot.

At last, Socrates speaks: 'Have you considered simply choosing to be sexy?'
His eighteen-months-on-testosterone stubble bristles with wisdom and
I ignore him.
'Oh fine, we'll do a dialectic then. Let's consider the antithetical.'

   Gender, yes! Woman, cold.

I like to perform my gender with great specificity
and enthusiasm. I confess my sins kneeling before
the door of a single-sex public bathroom, and draw
secondary sexual characteristics on images
of cartoon mice. Nearby,
a woman is slowly succumbing to
the onset of hypothermia. I cannot give
her my potentially life-saving puffer jacket
because I got it from the men's rack at a popular fast-fashion retailer.

   Gender, hot! Woman? No.

We like to throw a gender reveal party
every Friday night . . . . if you know what I mean.
No ladies allowed! Leave your wives at home!!
We sun ourselves like lizards in the heat and get ready
to fuck in the rhythms of our societally dictated sexual roles.
Then we usually go home because
no one will surrender their grip on hegemonic masculinity
long enough to have an orgasm.

    Gender? Maybe. Woman, of indeterminate temperature.

The doctor hefts the newborn in their gore-covered,
latex-gloved hands, and peers at the genital configuration.
'Yeah, I guess?' they shrug. The baby's mother
unhinges her jaw and devours the medical professional
for their impudence.

    Anti-gender? No. Man, hot.

As Gregor Samsa awoke one morning from uneasy dreams
she found herself transformed in her bed into a cisgender heterosexual.
'What has happened to me?' she thought. This was no dream.

    Gender, not-no. Woman, not-hot.

The woman loses track of herself inside the negatives.
'Am I here?' she asks.
'Am I here?'
'Am I here?' the nonbinary lesbian echoes like a call disconnecting.
Socrates emerges from the sea,
and opens his arms to the
undulating spill of the skies.
'Have you ever considered asking fewer questions?'

Driver's licence

My Uber driver is brushing his teeth
as we scrawl over Mount Victoria,

I shift solitary inside his strange interior,
wondering 'who am I to tell him what to do?'
Within the confines of his own car??

Life gets away from you
when the poetic potential of amphibious life-forms
is fully considered.

So I make another bargain with myself
to learn to drive
             properly this time
practical and diligent
unafraid to lose my way
through the back streets

hands splayed wide
against the seat
like the toes of an axolotl, pale and pinked,
and I can't help but think
neoteny means that the axolotl
reaches sexual maturity without
undergoing metamorphosis

             now, now I am a model organism
heart beating translucent under hands
with gloves snapped tight at the wrist
at a loss
for what it is that makes a person
want to stab hormones into an axolotl

translucent trembling like a gland
and is it the same urge that makes
me wonder

         what could become of me
if I could move through my body and
come out

         the other side

         like . . . .

when they shipped the axolotl
across the Atlantic
from Mexico City

         to the *Jardin des Plantes*

and Auguste Duméril opened the box
to find terrestrial salamanders
where the axolotl should have been.

Our ride evens around my corner,
and the Uber driver leans his body from the window

to smooth his hair
in the driver-side wing

with unearned, five-star confidence.

Love poem for the mustard yellow jacket I lost on TradeMe

I found you twenty-four pages deep in the vintage
category, seam to seam with a thousand tired florals.
Just my size, and egg-yolk yellow, and I am
all at once infatuated with a depth and profundity
that completely overshadows my ability to coordinate you
with my existing wardrobe choices.

You look like a jacket that will tell me you love
me, just three weeks and twenty-four pages in   (talk about a $1 reserve),
but you and your 70% wool blend
are boyfriend-material warm, semi-
waterproof and generous
around my thighs.

You will laugh about how I like The Smiths
even though you like bluegrass and EDM
and I can already tell that you will forget
my birthdays while you recount to me the plots
of films I will never see,
and you won't even be embarrassed by the
stereotypically masculine behaviour
that you are replicating in our upsettingly hetero dynamic.

. . .

Autobid just isn't a viable substitute
for being fully present,
but the fact that I only bid up to $15.50 suggests that I wasn't
ready for the kind of hard work necessary
in sustaining a long-term commitment
          to yellow jackets.

So I shouldn't feel too bad when someone comes along with a fatal $16.00
and a willingness to listen to you practise the accordion and talk about the holocaust,
because I was tired of being responsible for everything, and you shouldn't need
another person to make you better even though we all need other people to make us
better and the real problem is that you started making me worse and I didn't want to
do it anymore,

but my mum still cried when I told her I left you.

The pain is loosely equivalent to
catching my nipple in the hinge
as I slip into the shower.

I take a moment to feel everything,
and another to close the door.

Date idea: you commit a crime and then I hunt you relentlessly for seventeen years in the single-minded pursuit of bringing you to justice

we pound the pavements of the nineteenth century
       and I collect catches of you in long lit shadows
           in fragments of song
               across the faces of clocks

I want to ruin you in the Rue Montmartre
       throw you against the wall of some institution
         and cover your throat with my hands
             the lambent glow of barely repressed homoeroticism

       alight in our every move, and
this I swear by the stars I will find you in a moment of vulnerability
           (announcing myself via musical motif linked melodically to
              your trauma)
           in order to most effectively degrade
         your humanity, I will take your name from you
      replacing it with the swallowed hiss
of cold mathematics

       you can threaten me with violence in return,
         reluctantly at first, then with feeling
           all the whispered promise of your superior physical presence
             welling through the string section

       and then
     when the horns come in

I'll know you really mean it . . . .
          God

I want to be so stern and uncompromising for you

I want to re-enact my inability to form
                              healthy attachments

each time we meet
                    repeat

our own names like a talisman

        like a pathology

My name
        is Jean Valjean

                                        And I am Javert!
                                        Do not forget my name!

                            Do
                                not
                                    forget
                                            me

it's
        romantic as fuck

to be honest

        like

a thousand first dates

        a thousand ways to hold your wretched mouth

between my teeth

every time, you are new to me

scientists call it

'misattribution of arousal'

which is when your body sends you a little note to say
it's pretty sure you're about to die . . . .

only your reading comprehension isn't great

but personally, I like to call it

FATE

as you and I

my treasured enemy

make vow to one another

in perfect unison

I swear to you

I will be there

Gender of the Day

a shoebill, or
a piece of string,
those thumbnail frogs,
meandering,
a warehouse full of long-tailed bats,
the twitter feeds of technocrats,
the sound of rain on a bike,
unopened message from my psych,
a sky, a screech, a
pig on the beach,
debt forgiveness
out of reach,
an orange peel,
an earnest callout
Danielle Steele's ermine ball gown

Eryximachus on the erotic life of plants

Spring opens like an eyelid and
spreads its knees like margarine

the path down the stairs to my flat
erupts into a cicada sex dungeon

the breeze is running its fingers
along the spine of the forest,

petals open and
stamens erect,

a great crescendo of
screaming birds.

Hydrangeas are similar to humans
because they reproduce . . . . . . sexually.

Untouched in a mercurial year
I want to lick the salt from the spring rains
and adopt a new yoga routine and
steal a baby out of the back seat of a car

I am alive alive alive!

'Agapanthus is a prolific seeder'

bandying its deviant lifestyle choices
about the whole ecosystem.

Disgusting.

Love poem for the snail in our toilet

The cursed thing unfurls itself
slowly
like a tongue
in a porcelain mouth

'Just take it out' everyone says,
like it's easy
except that you have to hold him
like you love him

cradle him in the webbed space
between thumb and forefinger
between curled lip
and compassion

I can't do it but you can
I'm so lucky
that you love small
and terrible
things

Aristophanes at the contact centre

When I am nineteen, I presume
that by thirty-five I will own a house,
and a car, a savings account, a skincare routine,
a tasteful assortment of mid-range cheese in the fridge . . .
I presume

that I will spend my summers
growing organic produce;
tomatoes, cucumbers, beets and beans,
and I will have a fiddle-leaf fig, named Immanuel,
who will thrive perennially, despite any small incompetence on my part.

But sometimes, when I plant a kiss on his wide, waxy leaves,
I will remember being nineteen
on the first day of my worst job,
when a customer called our office to masturbate to the strain of my polite inquiries
as to the question of his purpose and identity.

It begins in a wave,
colleagues' calls clicking dead
in sequence as they've said
'Good morning,' my screen lights up
like a grin

and I wonder then, if the precipice of
each moment could be stretched
thin, laid flat and recategorised
into a series of decisions –
ordered numerically for

easy access – would this improve
things? I begin to see patterns

tapped across the expanse of
distance and time and I wonder
what he hears when I speak

press 1 to listen to your recent transactions
press 2 to sexually harass an intern

I am not unaccustomed
to violence, but nevertheless,
I begin to panic,
suspended like a circus act
at the very edge of my ACC coverage.

Ill-suited to employment, 'too sensitive'
and I worry that I have tricked him
somehow
into believing I am someone that
I am not.

press 1 to have an appropriate reaction to your experiences
press 2 to tell this man that you cannot help him if he does
not provide you with his customer number

I imagine telling him that he has
made some sort of mistake, because
he was probably looking for someone else –
someone specific, with whom
he has a pre-established relationship,

where they call each other at work
and then get off in the bathroom or something –
and he is mortified by the misunderstanding
but because I am so resilient and generous of spirit and
also I never dwell on things, we laugh together and he says

haha, oh what excellent service and sense of personal connection you have provided!
can I see you again?

and I tell him that unfortunately I am on a weekly roster
and have no control over my time
but I hope he has a lovely day

and then I receive accolades and
a promotion and free mental health support
and I never have to work in a call centre again.

I will not cry today, but I will the next day.
I will cry about Immanuel Kant's formulation
of humanity, which goes like this:

no person should be used as a means to an end,
but only as an end in themselves

and in a year or so,
I will break up with the
Okay Boyfriend
that I am in love with
and some time, some

year down the line,
I will have an indoor plant named Immanuel,
and I will worry that I am running out of time
as I pour a saucerful of water over his roots
and whisper

is this enough?

All my plants are dead and I'm pretty sure it's your fault

I think it's extremely inconsiderate of you, showing up and being exactly the sort of person that I would become immediately obsessed with.

The planet is dying and so is my half-price orchid from Bunnings

and you don't even care and neither do I.

If we were in a real poem probably all my plants would be doing fine, despite my emotionally distant behaviour.

Because they would understand how I feel and bloom harder instead of dying and also they would smell like the concept of lesbians.

Sometimes life furnishes you with imperfect metaphors to complement your assortment of low-maintenance house plants that,

as it turns out, aren't quite low maintenance enough.

But telling you how I feel about you in a poem is like blurting out 'I love you' at a three way:

my audience isn't sure who I'm talking to, and no one involved can tell if I mean it or not.

What I'm trying to say is that it isn't totally your fault that I like you so much that I started neglecting all of my usual responsibilities just so

I could watch nature documentaries in your shitty apartment,

but taking responsibility for my own failings as a person is very hard,

and flirting with you in a playfully accusatory tone at a suitably ironic distance through the medium of literature is very easy.

So my hyacinth curls like an old fingernail,

my basil pot and related Italian-home-cooking fantasies wither prematurely into dust,

and my zebra plant lives so close to the verge of extinction that David Attenborough is raising awareness in one last Netflix special.

My cactuses are doing okay, but sometimes they get a little critical when I come in late with two shades of lipstick on my teeth.

'Don't you care about the environment?' they bristle, spines in the shapes of rhetorical question marks.

'All of the bees are dying and no one cares if you're in love or not except you.'

Love poem asking you to come to bed with me (as a friend though haha)

I try on all your red dresses
because we have decided to pretend

we are Kate Bush à la 'Wuthering Heights'
my teeth hurt from laughing

and I am performatively furious
that none of them look as good on me as they do on you

red just isn't my colour
or maybe my judgement is compromised

because I'm half in love with you
(just kidding)

I want to kiss the space above your collarbone
but like, platonically, I guess

I want to talk about our hypothetical future
the chickens that will scratch in our hypothetical garden

your fingers close around my wrist
like parentheses

(oh no)
so I run alongside you like a current

until the other side of 2 a.m.
when your lashes dip below the water line

you climb into my bed
and curl around me like a question mark

I don't need an answer
to wake up breathing your air

in a yellow parallelogram
of sunlight

Agathon tries to locate the image

Today I tried to do better,
but it wasn't working.
Every one of my thoughts
was very stupid,

and all the hours went stale
as I scaled them. So I went
to my favourite place,
to see if I could find it

the sound of
the thing, the ring
as everything clicks into place
like a box closing.

Now I stand on the pavement
next to the clothes bank,
where the cars parked parallel
are filled with spills of garbage.

I gather their shapes to me:
the silhouette of bin bags, and
sneakers tied in grey, the scrape
of ratty backpacks,

the outline of a
Toyota FunCargo
packed with flax.
But, today, two men

are here before me.
So I hang back

as one stacks the truck with spoils,
and the other sorts through the rubble

of blankets and cardboard damp.
He pulls a hard case from the
refuse, scuffed, and as long as a shin.
Oi, look at this!

The case clicks awake in his palms.
He lifts the quarter-sized banjo
. . . experimentally, as
light settles in the bones of his smile.

Ekphrasis (I am transforming into a sexy anthropomorphic mouse and no one can stop me)

After Osamu Tezuka

after they set the key to the lock,
everything turns clockwise with a click
and i appear with a sigh
the drawer shyly unstuck

the drawn curve of my spine
held soft in the sheets
of a languid and unfamiliar
country

in eggshell cream folded fine
i waited
the sight of me secret
an absence

now licked
into place
with a dab
of my firm little tongue

Ten thousand digital ghosts in my pants

It takes six months of algorithms trying to sell me
birth control and beardscaping before I realise

there is more than one of me in there

and the realisation looks like a white room
of frantic telemarketers comparing notes
on my search history   *do* mushrooms have sex?
And then half of them conclude I need a pregnancy test
and the other half decide that I am a man
who is looking for love
                                        in all the wrong places.

I watch them go through it, these shadow
selves, as I move from room to room,
conclusions lengthening in the afternoon sun
haemorrhoid cream to early childcare –
it makes me want to tell my pregnant ghost
that we can still do prenatal yoga sometimes
if it would make her happy
. . . but probably not every day

and as for him, I think,
beard oil download Tinder today
a romantic getaway, a diamond ring
            Hinge? (a tragedy in five parts)
            . . . .
                        I hope he's okay

it feels less lonely, to think there are thousands of
me out there
buying yoga mats and Spotify Premium

and that we might all still be connected, somehow
despite our wildly different lifestyle choices

honestly, it's kind of a relief for a moment,
it's too hard to be a person with any sort of consistency,

and sometimes I want to outsource my identity
transmute my body into data
lie down in the moss
and hand everything over to the ghosts.

Love poem for the space you ought to occupy

often, when I think about loving you
I think that I want to write about it

squash your face into the confines of an old-fashioned locket
heavy with brass and significance

like coiling a knot of hair around my little finger
or keeping an eyelash in a tin

I need to do this, in case everyone missed it
somehow, that you have a universe inside you

sprawling wide and wise, in deliberate vastness, and that
sometimes, I can even dangle my legs over the edge

marvelling at all the colours of your
entire visible light spectrum

Zeno's paradox posits that infinities exist between all of us
and so the motion of drawing closer is a kind of fiction

and I feel that, sometimes, in the aching yawn
of distance across *what are you thinking* and breakfast

so instead of anything coherent I say
you are the opposite of a monologue about trains

and these are the times when I think about
how you never asked to be a 'you' in a poem

impossibly contained in
an amateur cosmic terrarium

is it enough to love the absence
of certainty?

how many old photographs there must be,
holes cut heart-shape

across the throats of people
who are loved

You're welcome, from Plato

After Anne Carson

It was on the third day of a lockdown when our kettle died. It seems frivolous to say *died*, under the circumstances, but it was one of those days that blows through and leaves you lacking. I had already been on Twitter to complain, so the time had come to do something about it, only I wasn't sure what, so instead I sat down with Plato and asked what was going on with him. I will ask you to bear with me, I do have a Philosophy degree, but I probably shouldn't. Anyway, instead of giving me a direct answer to my question, Plato staged an elaborate dialogue between Socrates and a cohort of his contemporaries, where they all expounded on the nature of the linguistic specificities of the phrase 'what's going on' from the comfort of my woolly green armchair. Plato works like ancient experimental theatre – he writes all the lines, refuses to play any of the roles, and then mashes everyone together like dolls until the truth falls out. I suspect that Plato is a maximalist. Unfortunately, it made me nervous to approach him on the topic of love, which is what I had really been hoping to get into. I've always thought that *Symposium*, the dialogue on love, was the good one. It delighted me that it didn't seem concerned with squeezing answers out of binaries. Instead the seven speeches are sung, none quite in total opposition, the meanings jostling gently alongside one another in the space between what is known and what is just slightly beyond knowing. So, I put my big lumpy jumper on over my leggings, cracked open my door, and moved mustily into the road. Then I kept moving. I moved through meandering hills, the bus tunnel, a ridge along water. I took a moment to think 'it is good that all the cars have stopped moving' and then passed the houses of the wealthy, rising like teeth, as I stomped down to the water's edge. The water tapped pleasingly along the shoreline but the beach itself was deeply unromantic, sagging jetty full of seagull splatter, DANGER please keep off, seaweed clogging the boat ramp. I sat on a log and waited until my hands got cold, dreaming of the hot cup of tea I couldn't have. There was an oystercatcher perched on a rock in the water and I wrote this down. I worried then, that I was trying to manufacture meaning out of an oystercatcher. Then I worried that I wasn't doing a good job of it. There is a twinge in me that wants to reach further than I can, to tether moments together like constellations, to see the place at which something disparate begins to touch the points at which they all connect. I imagine us all like molecules pressing ourselves against a membrane, searching for a pulse, finding something pressing back. The wind changes, boats creaking in the near distance and stumpy waves sounding against the shore, breaking over brick and the concrete husks of the things underneath. The oystercatcher flaps, surprised, and the mumble of cars fades in the face of this. I remember last spring when I saw tiny fish in these waters, flashing in the shallows, and I think about the ways we learn to survive. I think about this ugly beach and how, even if it's not easy to love it, I think it's worth trying – maybe I should tell Plato. I don't know if I know what it means to love, but I know that when I open my body like a question, I am laid tenderly along the hum of the seams of everything else there is. I think about existing not as a finite thing, but as a string of moments through time. I think about how now that I have stood here, this ugly beach is a part of me, and how maybe when it is spring, all of the silver fish will come back. I think about the purpose of dialogue and the space between molecules. I think of everything that we have all endured and I think of looking back through the mesh of time and memory and the empty things inside me and saying 'none of me would be here without you.'

III

ALCIBIADES CHOOSES THEIR OWN ADVENTURE

You Are Alcibiades

It's 10 p.m. and you are standing in front of a sink,
sequin bikini set rustling like prayer beads and
cheap red pulsing in your wrists
the dress code for where you're supposed to be
is 'slutty pangender mermaid sex party'
and you always aim to please,

which is why you're in a bathroom
tweezing thick hairs from Ben's pale shoulder because
now that he's twenty-seven he's afraid
and twinks age faster than the tides
of time itself, so you sprinkle glitter on him when
you're done, because you're a good friend
and the holo glare of light on tile
makes you shine so wild
you could make swans cry

his boyfriend is still in England so he keeps
meeting men on Grindr just to
play board games and then ghost them, because
he's too radiant to be lonely, and you
understand the impulse to
create a fantasy of yourself, like reaching
across the sky
to run your fingertips along
an endless string of pearls
   until it all goes dark

> **Text the girl you've been thinking about (page 74)**
> **Absolutely do not fucking do that (page 75)**

Text the girl you've been thinking about

Hey sorry it's me haha / I want you /
to pay attention to me / please god /

I'm just / on my way to this party / and I sound like a
nerd in an Uber / which I am / I hope the writing is going

well / mine isn't / I keep thinking about the line / of your brow /
in the slant of morning / and how you like to type with your whole body /

feet flexing / shoulders furious / and how I like to type next to you /
in silence / usually I can't stand empty spaces /

empty pages / I know I said I'd wait / and see /
unfortunately / I didn't wait /

if this message had alt text / it would be in sonnet form/ if my fractal self /
couldn't pretend confidence for one night / what would be the point / lmao

just to let you know / I look hot / I'm covered in glitter /
and I wanna kiss you / again

> **Sexy dissociation (page 83)**
> **Rampant mania (page 84)**

Absolutely do not fucking do that

Do not panic
instead, you can pluck Ben until he is smooth
like a dolphin and cry about your shared religious trauma
on the kitchen floor
through great wide loops
of lyric time.

You do not have to
bake three separate cakes to bring
to this birthday party,
it's not that kind of party, and

you do not need
the components for chocolate buttercream
to be packed in neat oblongs, useless
as a cigarette case full of cicadas,

you should not bother
because they're not going to have a stand mixer
at the slutty pangender mermaid sex party
anyway.

You should eat something maybe
so you suck crumbs
from your palms and laugh in cryptic crossword
and avoid and avoid and avoid.

You should not wonder
if this is good intimacy because you're doing it
with a man or bad, narcissistic intimacy because you're
both exactly what they feared you'd be.

Look, do you want to be a Hot Girl
or not?

> **I don't know if I'm Hot? (page 77)**
> **I don't know if I'm a Girl? (page 79)**

Body dysmorphia is expensive and poetry is free

the thing is, you're hot now

so hot that you're basically irresistible   like an itch or something

hot hot hot

you are a wing beat   pulsing under the epidermis

hey babe, are you a particle physicist's wildest dream?
          because you're radiant as fuck   and no one can explain it!

your hotness is swelling dangerously
like a hen's crop
                    or a third breast

you're so hot you're hurting *everybody's* feelings

so hot you're almost coherent

. . . .

. . . you're so hot that people are attracted to you sometimes

you're so hot that people are attracted to you RIGHT NOW

the sea roars in your blood

and it is heating to dangerous and previously unrecorded levels you're so hot . . . . did you know?

. . . . you are so hot right now

> **You're right, my hotness is undeniable and I feel very empowered right now (page 81)**
> **I'm so hot that I should text that girl I've been thinking about (page 74)**

Gender is fake and so am I

I tell everyone that
I'm a Gemini
even though it's not really true,
and not everyone believes in cusps,
including me

but I do believe in multiplicity
and
let's be real for a second   . . . . even if
astrology was more   than an attempt
          to know and categorise the self
into neat   emotionally promising
and ultimately
          hollow houses
fixed and immovable,
like some celestial
              Harry Potter shit

you weren't going to get
          much further than
my rising sign   right?
      it'll be like
                  I never lied   at all

and what if   instead
it was a language
that you could only speak with dogs
at high tide under linked hands,
with the universe shining through

lot of significant Scorpio placements if you know what I mean

secret signals between, whispered
under, the mattresses of frivolity
atmospheres colliding
stars shining, eliding the boundaries,
and tangled in the string   of everything else

> **She doesn't care what gender you are you should text her (page 74)**
> **Dissociate . . . . sexily (page 83)**

I AM SO HOT THAT IT'S PROBABLY DISRUPTING THE SPACE-TIME CONTINUUM

After Olafur Eliasson

You no longer have use for the concept
of linearity. Instead you commit yourself
to intuitive, associative movements,
light exercise and anti-capitalist sentiment,

so that you're ready when the mists roll across the
mirrored surface of time, and the doors open in
spaceflight static. It makes a sound like a
microwave unfolding into the fourth dimension.

I am so hot right now

you think, as you enter the
Chamber of the Captive Sun. One
part positive affirmation,
two parts ontological statement

she rises before you, the sun, in a sea
of searing incandescence
and nuclear fusion, light spiked
across the entire visible spectrum

in the place where they keep her,
sinking slowly under
the weight of paid admission,
chained in weather,

the bodies of raptured saints
sprawling in the pull
of her tides of fire, and you weep as
she burns every trace of plastic memory right out

of the collective unconscious
in a single
solar
flare.

I am so fucking hot right now

> **Your body cannot withstand the temperature of the sun in such
> close proximity, regardless of whether or not the sun is a metaphor
> in this instance.
> You are dead.**

Alcibiades walks into a room

and it's like being on the inside
of a disco ball with tits.

The colours shift in waves
and faces shift like sand.

Your screen sits silent,
hollow as a heartbeat, and

your phone is in your hand,
and you would put it down,

except that there's no space
on your body

to hide anything
larger than a sequin.

> Time passes differently when you're waiting for a response to a
   text message. Thousands of years go by, civilisations rise and fall,
   and your mortal flesh twists and shrivels, dry as a stick.
   You are dead.

Everything is going to be fine forever

I can tell.

I can tell because I've been to the future.
and I asked everyone there, personally.

They told me that it all works out,
and then they cured my depression.

I explain this to the people around me,
gesturing with wild, wispy hands.
My hair is plastic-green like a poisonous frog and
I am amphibious, half-in and
half-out of every conversation
delirious with the sick, sweet smell of orchids,
triple-stacked air-fresheners in the back of the Uber
and vodka mixers, cranberry-sharp and syrupy.

I am in a photo booth of shining streamers
gold foil and fish scales,
in a hallway lined with neon balloons and simmering undercurrents
of queer desire I am in a bathroom with a shirtless merman
and his new nipple-piercing and I tell him that
it is very nice, and everything is going to be fine forever.

When I had my ears re-pierced
I went into a room alone with a man, his own
ears stretched wide and low, as if eggs
were set heavy in the lobes and he asked

me to take my shirt off so
I summoned all of my dignity and courage and
all I managed was *excuse me?*
but it turned out it wasn't sexual harassment
it was just a scheduling conflict,
and a woman who did want her nipples pierced
was sitting in the waiting room
drifting out of time and tangent
wondering why she had been waiting so long.

I wonder if I will ever know that feeling again,
submerged in a kitchen
with two indistinguishable women and
three unnecessary birthday cakes,
but the thought is sharp and clear and crisp like snow,

and it is then when you
sorry I'm late your way into the room

and I
hold your jaw between my hands and

crawl desperately back to land.

> **Maybe we should get a drink or something I hear the backyard is
   lovely this time of year (page 86)**
> **What if we fell in love and moved in together and got married
   but like in the future and again? (page 88)**

Bubble machine transforming into a metaphor

The hours coalesce
in honeyed specks of shine,
your hand in mine, as we lie
under stars and smoke rings.

Did Liam rent a bubble machine?
They float in spectral orbit,
cyan, pink and lucid blue smudged
across our line of sight,

and I wish we could reach for them
close our fingers together
balanced light but sure,
a thing delicate and dear

between them.
The light spins and
I am shucked
from our inflatable clamshell

a discount Aphrodite
with a hangover
that hasn't hit
the ground,

and I feel
hunger along my spine

in skim-milk trace
powder praying

wretched obeying
as you hold my hair
and tell me
I'm doing fine.

> You are so devastated by the consequences of your own decisions
and the way that they impact the people around you that you die.
You are dead.

But remember? Everything is going to be fine. (page 88)

Love poem for a future

In the future
my shirt is stretched tight across my belly.
I am round, and smooth
as the globe of a terrarium and when I tell you,
your mouth spills open like a sunrise.

In this future we
control our own narratives, and in this future I
am smug and full, like a parental fridge and
together, we will cross the threshold
and pledge a lifelong commitment to
the inherent lesbian eroticism of choosing furniture together
and Sunday mornings
and I, against all the odds, am radiant.

So let's scandalise my grandmother together,
let me weep openly at the altar
in honour of your eyebrows and
the lifetime of emotional fulfilment
that we are about to promise each other.

We'll kiss then, and everyone will burst
into spontaneous applause. And
I am still in my second-hand wedding dress, full,
and tired around the eyes as you
clutch my hand in the delivery room.

And after a tasteful montage
of heaving and crying
and breathing and
I'm almost there,
it's coming!

Your hands are on my body
and soon,
a friendly cactus emerges
from my abdomen,
damp with blood, and
crowned with light.

Notes

The quote from Leo Strauss originates from *On Plato's Symposium*, reproduced with
   permission from Chicago University Press.
   Seth Benardete (ed.), *Leo Strauss On Plato's Symposium*, University of Chicago Press,
      Chicago, 2001, p. 11.

The definition of 'Symposium' in '*Symposium* (Adapted)' is provided by the Oxford
   Languages website https://languages.oup.com. The characters and structure of the
   poem are interpretations of the characters and structure of Plato's *Symposium*.

'Phaedrus' is an erasure poem, taken and modified from Phaedrus's speech in Plato's
   Symposium (Robin Waterfield, trans., Oxford University Press, Oxford, 1994).
   '~~SOCRATES~~ CORRECT' contains excerpts from Socrates' speech.

'Goodreads accessing the communal mind to deliver a balanced review of Plato's
   Symposium (385–370 BCE)' is a found poem collaged from user reviews of
   The Symposium on Goodreads: www.goodreads.com/book/show/81779.The_
   Symposium

'Phaedrus Recites a Catalogue of Ships' contains a refrain taken from the catalogue of
   ships in Homer's *The Iliad* (Richard Lattimore, trans., Book 2, pp. 493–518, University
   of Chicago Press, Chicago, 1951). This poem also contains research adapted from the
   following academic papers:
   Deborah N. Carlson, 'Seeing the Sea: Ships' Eyes in Classical Greece', *Hesperia: The
      Journal of the American School of Classical Studies at Athens*, 78(3), 2009, 347–65.
   Aaron L. Mishara, 'Klaus Conrad (1905–1961): Delusional Mood, Psychosis, and
      Beginning Schizophrenia', *Schizophrenia Bulletin*, 36(1), 2010, 9–13.

'Gender, no. Woman, hot: A Dialectic Executed to Reveal the Nonbinary Lesbian'
   contains a stanza adapted from Franz Kafka's *Metamorphosis* (Nahum Glatzer, ed.,
   The Complete Stories, Schocken Books, New York, 1971). Available at: www.sas.upenn.
   edu/~cavitch/pdf-library/Kafka_Metamorphosis.pdf

'Driver's licence' refers to the neoteny of the axolotl, researched variously and with poetic
   licence from some dubious sources. But here's a good one:
   Christian Reiß, Lennart Olsson and Uwe Hoßfeld, 'The History of the Oldest

Self-sustaining Laboratory Animal: 150 Years of Axolotl Research', *Journal of Experimental Zoology*, 324(5), 2015, 393–465. Available at: https://doi.org/10.1002/jez.b.22617

'Date idea: you commit a crime and then I hunt you relentlessly for seventeen years in the single-minded pursuit of bringing you to justice' is shameless fanfiction of the stage musical adaptation of Victor Hugo's *Les Misérables* by Claude-Michel Schönberg, including quotes and fragments from the musical numbers 'Work Song', 'Stars' and 'The Confrontation'.

'Gender of the Day' contains interpretations of memes that my friends have sent me, and owes its title to Twitter bot, genderoftheday: https://twitter.com/genderoftheday

'Agathon tries to locate the image' adapts a line from the letters of W. B. Yeats to Dorothy Wellesley, 8 September 1935, '[A] poem comes right with a click like a closing box.' William Butler Yeats and Dorothy Wellesley, *Letters on Poetry from W. B. Yeats to Dorothy Wellesley*, Oxford University Press, Oxford, 1964, p. 22.

'Ekphrasis (I am transforming into a sexy anthropomorphic mouse and no one can stop me)' was written in response to Osamu Tezuka's sketches, seen here: https://archive.org/details/erotica_of_osamu_tezuka

'I AM SO HOT THAT IT'S PROBABLY DISRUPTING THE SPACE-TIME CONTINUUM' was written in response to *The Weather Project* (2003) by Olafur Eliasson: https://olafureliasson.net/archive/artwork/WEK101003/the-weather-project

Previous Publications

Thank you to all the editors of the following journals and websites.

'You are . . . ERYXIMACHUS' and 'Date idea: you commit a crime and then I hunt you relentlessly for seventeen years in the single-minded pursuit of bringing you to justice' were first published in *Sweet Mammalian*.

'Pausanias Explains My Sexuality to Me' was first published by *Bad Apple*.

'Gender, no. Woman, hot: A Dialectic Executed to Reveal the Nonbinary Lesbian' and 'All my plants are dead and I'm pretty sure it's your fault' originally appeared on *The Spinoff*.

'Gender of the Day' was originally published in *Turbine | Kapohau*.

'Eryximachus on the erotic life of plants' and 'Love poem asking you to come to bed with me (as a friend though haha)' were both originally published in *takahē*.

'Everything is going to be fine forever' was published in *Stasis Journal*.

Acknowledgements

Writing a book is, as it turns out, very difficult. And this particular book wouldn't exist without the support I received from a frankly staggering number of people, some of whom I will now try to thank. (The execution of this task will not be adequate to express the depth of my gratitude.)

Thank you to Anna Jackson, who supported me through the writing process with patience, generosity and the most marvellous book recommendations. Thank you to Helen Rickerby for your excellent feedback, and also for being right about everything. Thank you also to Rebecca Hawkes for your kind words. Your excerpts from the Emperors New Groove meme group haunt me to this day. Eternal thanks to Sam, Sophia and the whole team at AUP for making this book a reality, to Emma Neale for being a brilliant editor and a delight to correspond with, to Louise Belcher for proofreading and Amy Tansell for the internal design. And to Philip for an excellent cover.

Thank you to the wonderful MA workshop of 2021 – Jiaqiao, Leah, Lachlan, Zoe, Scarlett, Sylvan, Bronte, Flora and Maggie. Your work has continued to inspire me. Thank you to poetry club. I'm so grateful to have a community in which to read, write, perform and occasionally set a table on fire. Thank you to Chris Price, you have forever changed the way I punctuate. Thank you James, Damien, Kate, Tina, Katie and Claire and everyone else at the IIML, for providing a space to read, work and enjoy many poetry-related breakdowns. Thank you Ian for being such a supportive manager while I was trying to write this book. And thank you, too, to the team at Wellington City Archives. It has been very nice of my various jobs to be so kind to me while I was deranged on poetry.

The cover concept was taken from a maniacal, late-night Google image search, which turned up a Reddit thread about Pradier's *Les Trois Grâces* with the dicks lovingly Photoshopped on. Thank you to the internet strangers who made this possible (I wish we could've found you), and thank you very much to Bo Moore for creating the Richer adaptation that features on this cover.

Abundant thanks is owed to my astonishingly brilliant friends, who read my manuscripts more than once, and answered questions such as 'Do you think the form achieves the philosophical aims of the project?' and 'Am I a total wanker?' with patience, grace and insight. Thank you particularly (again) to Bo Moore, who let me crouch freakishly in her house during the editing process, and who likes to tell me she doesn't know anything about poetry before giving me astute and practical feedback. Thank you to Tara, Sam and David, for letting me infiltrate drawing club with my laptop. Thank you to Rowan, for always making time to read my work. I'm sorry that I made you into Socrates in that first draft. Moth, it has been such a delight sharing poems with you. Jem, thank you for everything, but especially for that time you fished a snail out of a toilet so I didn't have to. Hannah, it was very kind of you to read my book, and also very kind of you to be my roommate back in 2010, when I was barely human. Lovely Ben, you are so clever and helpful. I hope you held off reading this so you could properly enjoy the French Riviera.

I owe much love and thanks to all of the friends and family who have supported me, and especially to the ones who (very generously) did not read my book, thereby forcing me to have something else to talk about, sometimes. Thank you to Zelle, Sammy, Renée and family. Much love to my sister Alex. To my mum, and gran and everyone else. Thank you to the Bollingers and McRaes – Nick, Kathy, Elsie, Etta, Rona, Alyson, Matt and Elizabeth – for always making me feel welcome.

To Sally. Thank you for your warmth and integrity and cleverness, and for making the world better than it was before.

Dani Yourukova is 'a queer Wellington writer with great hair and a bad personality' who completed their MA at Te Herenga Waka—Victoria University of Wellington. Their work has been published in *takahē, Stasis, The Spinoff, Turbine | Kapohau* and the *Poetry New Zealand Yearbook.*